Smoothies

The 30 Day Smoothie Revelation: The Best 30 Smoothie Recipes On Earth, 1 Recipe for Every Day of the Month

The 30 Day Smoothie Revelation

The Best 30 Smoothie Recipes On Earth, 1 Recipe for Every Day of the Month

By: Vanessa Williams

Preface

First of all, let me tell you how happy I am for downloading my book. "**Smoothies - The 30 Day Smoothie Revelation: The Best 30 Smoothie Recipes On Earth, 1 Recipe for Every Day of the Month**".

Inside this book, I tried to include 30 of the best smoothie recipes I have tried during the past years. I am a big fan of smoothies my self and I always try to learn and try new recipes for my friends and me. I cannot tell you how many nights we have worked out, based on smoothies alone.

So every time I tried a new recipe I liked I noted down in my "big smoothie recipe book". I have collected over 100 smoothie recipes over the years, and I finally decided to present to you the best 30...err...35 of them. They are categorized based on my favorite fruits, plus some of the best green smoothies as a detox 5 day plan.

As you are going to find out, in every recipe, I tried to keep the ingredients as easy and non-expensive as possible because I wanted the recipes to be fast to make with minimum cost...but all the fan and taste!

Moreover I calculated the calories you get from every recipe, and the exact nutrients and I presented them in a very informative and easy to read table.

Thanks again for downloading this book, I hope you enjoy it!

Table of Contents

Introduction

Smoothies have become the next big thing due to their convenience and the amount of punch they pack when it comes to nutrients. The average smoothie will have your daily dose of vitamin C, along with many other invaluable vitamins that you need daily. Plus, they taste really great!

In this book, you'll find thirty-five smoothie recipes that will surely make your taste buds tingle and your body thank you for the delicious, healthy meal (or snack). Don't forget to take a peek at the dessert section! You'll be surprised by the low amount of calories and carbs in these delightful smoothies.

Chapter One – Green Smoothies

Made popular through the seven-day green smoothie diet, these smoothies are an excellent choice to add your arsenal of cleansing smoothies. They're also great just because they taste good, too!

Kale and Banana Smoothie

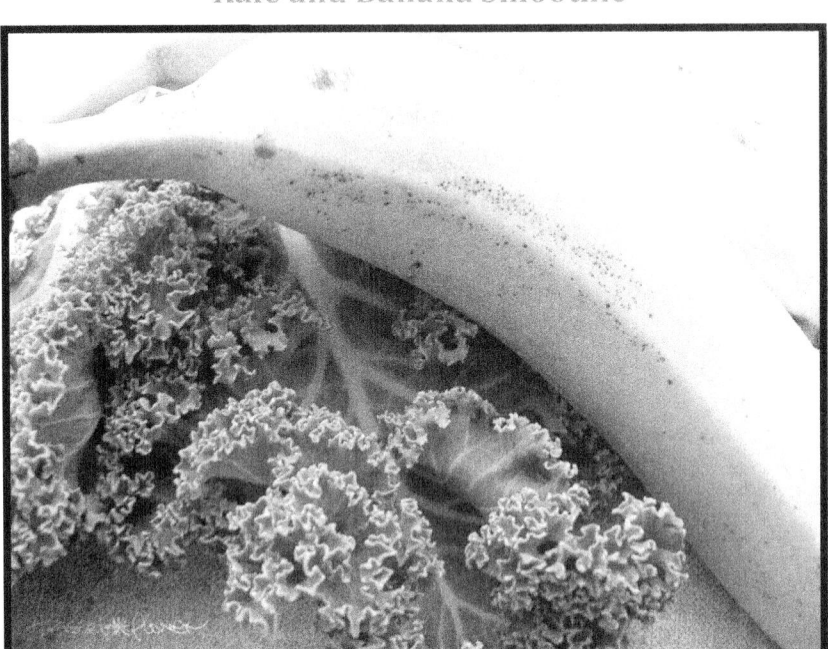

Photo courtesy of Mervi Eskelinen at Flickr.com

Servings: 1

Prep: 5 Minutes

Ready In: 5 Minutes

Ingredients

- 1 Banana
- 2 C. Chopped Kale

- ½ C. Soy Milk
- 1 Tbsp. Flax Seed
- 1 tsp. Maple Syrup

Directions

1. Place the ingredients in the blender and cover. Puree until it's smooth and serve over ice with a straw.

Nutritional Information

Serving Size: 1 Recipe

Calories: 311

Calories from Fat: 66

Nutrient	Grams/mg	% Based on 2,000 Calorie Diet
Total Fat	7.3g	11%
Saturated Fat	0.8g	4%
Cholesterol	0mg	0%
Sodium	110mg	4%
Potassium	1294mg	36%
Total Carbohydrates	56.6g	18%
Dietary Fiber	10.1g	40%
Protein	12.2g	24%
Sugars	21.2g	
Vitamin A		424%
Vitamin C		290%
Calcium		44%
Iron		44%
Thiamin		22%
Niacin		32%
Vitamin B6		58%
Magnesium		45%
Folate		48%

Kale Orange Banana Smoothie

Photo courtesy of Desmond Talkington at Flickr.com

Servings: 1

Prep: 10 Minutes

Ready In: 10 Minutes

Ingredients

- 1 Orange
- ½ C. Water
- 1 Kale Leaf
- 2 Bananas, Peeled

Directions

1. Place the kale and water in the blender first and pulse until smooth.
2. Add the remaining two ingredients and pulse until smooth.

Nutritional Information

Serving Size: 1 Recipe

Calories: 220

Calories from Fat: 8

Nutrient	Grams/mg	% Based on 2,000 Calorie Diet
Total Fat	0.9g	1%
Saturated Fat	0.3g	1%
Cholesterol	0mg	0%
Sodium	15mg	<1%
Potassium	935mg	26%
Total Carbohydrates	55.9g	18%
Dietary Fiber	6.5g	26%
Protein	3.2g	6%
Sugars	28.9g	
Vitamin A		65%
Vitamin C		74%
Calcium		5%
Iron		10%
Thiamin		13%

Niacin		17%
Vitamin B6		58%
Magnesium		26%
Folate		29%

Cinnamon Apple Smoothie

Photo courtesy of Haniela at Flickr.com

Servings: 2

Prep: 10 Minutes

Ready In: 10 Minutes

Ingredients

- 1 C. Apple Juice
- 1 Pear, Cored and Sliced
- 1 Apple, Cored and Sliced
- 1 C. Spinach

- 1 tsp. Cinnamon, Ground
- ½ C. Ice

Directions

1. Place the spinach and apple juice in first and blend until smooth.
2. Add the remainder of the ingredients and pulse until smooth.

Nutritional Information

Serving Size: ½ Recipe

Calories: 249

Calories from Fat: 4

Nutrient	Grams/mg	% Based on 2,000 Calorie Diet
Total Fat	0.4g	<1%
Saturated Fat	0.1g	<1%
Cholesterol	0mg	0%
Sodium	19mg	<1%
Potassium	409mg	11%
Total Carbohydrates	38.3g	12%
Dietary Fiber	5.3g	21%
Protein	1g	2%
Sugars	28.9g	
Vitamin A		29%
Vitamin C		20%
Calcium		6%
Iron		12%
Thiamin		7%
Niacin		5%
Vitamin B6		7%
Magnesium		9%
Folate		21%

Jumping Ginger Smoothie

Photo courtesy of Tasty Yummies at Flickr.com

Servings: 1

Prep: 10 Minutes

Ready In: 10 Minutes

Ingredients

- 2 C. Water
- 1 Avocado
- ½ C. Parsley
- 1 Apple
- 1 Carrot
- 1 Lemon
- 1 Kale Leaf
- 1" Fresh Ginger
- 2 Ice Cubes
- 1 Tbsp. Flaxseed

Directions

1. Place the water, kale and parsley into the blender and pulse until smooth.
2. Place the remainder of the ingredients in the blender and run until smooth.
3. Place ice and flaxseed in if desired.

Nutritional Information

Serving Size: 1 Recipe

Calories: 530

Calories from Fat: 321

Nutrient	Grams/mg	% Based on 2,000 Calorie Diet
Total Fat	35.7g	55%
Saturated Fat	4.9g	24%
Cholesterol	0mg	0%
Sodium	106mg	4%
Potassium	1862mg	52%
Total Carbohydrates	62.4g	20%
Dietary Fiber	28.5g	114%
Protein	10.1g	20%
Sugars	19.1g	
Vitamin A		324%
Vitamin C		301%
Calcium		30%
Iron		52%
Thiamin		43%
Niacin		56%
Vitamin B6		58%
Magnesium		58%
Folate		138%

Green Power Mojito Smoothie

Photo courtesy of Shekhar Mehta at Flickr.com

Servings: 4

Prep: 10 Minutes

Ready In: 10 Minutes

Ingredients

- 3 C. Ice
- 2 C. Spinach
- 7 oz. Crushed Pineapple
- ½ C. Water
- 1 Banana
- 1 Orange
- 10 Mint Leaves
- 1 Lemon

- 1 Lime

Directions

1. Juice the lemon and the lime.
2. Place the fruit juices and water in the blender with the mint leaves and spinach and pulse until smooth.
3. Place in the remainder of the ingredients in the blender and blend until smooth.

Nutritional Information

Serving Size: ¼ Recipe

Calories: 94

Calories from Fat: 2

Nutrient	Grams/mg	% Based on 2,000 Calorie Diet
Total Fat	0.3g	<1%
Saturated Fat	0.1g	<1%
Cholesterol	0mg	0%
Sodium	19mg	<1%
Potassium	372mg	10%
Total Carbohydrates	24.2g	8%
Dietary Fiber	2.7g	11%
Protein	1.5g	3%
Sugars	17.4g	
Vitamin A		31%
Vitamin C		72%
Calcium		6%
Iron		7%
Thiamin		7%
Niacin		7%
Vitamin B6		14%
Magnesium		13%
Folate		30%

Chapter Two – Banana Smoothies

High in potassium, the banana is a great addition to any smoothie because it gives it that extra creamy texture. Be sure to use ripe bananas and freeze them if you'd like a little extra thickness.

Banana, Blueberry, and Peanut Butter Smoothie

Photo courtesy of Reya Veltman at Flickr.com

Servings: 2

Prep: 10 Minutes

Ready In: 10 Minutes

Ingredients

- 1 Tbsp. Flaxseed
- 1 Banana
- ½ C. Frozen Blueberries
- 1 Tbsp. Peanut Butter

- 1 tsp. Honey
- ½ C. Yogurt
- 1 C. Milk

Directions

1. Place all ingredients in the blender and pulse until smooth.

Nutritional Information

Serving Size: ½ Recipe

Calories: 251

Calories from Fat: 83

Nutrient	Grams/mg	% Based on 2,000 Calorie Diet
Total Fat	9.2g	14%
Saturated Fat	3.2g	16%
Cholesterol	13mg	4%
Sodium	132mg	5%
Potassium	649mg	18%
Total Carbohydrates	34.4g	11%
Dietary Fiber	3.9g	15%
Protein	10.8g	22%
Sugars	24.7g	
Vitamin A		6%
Vitamin C		16%
Calcium		34%
Iron		7%
Thiamin		13%
Niacin		27%
Vitamin B6		23%
Magnesium		24%
Folate		20%

Apple Banana Smoothie

Photo courtesy of Derryn_NZ at Flickr.com

Servings: 2

Prep: 10 Minutes

Ready In: 10 Minutes

Ingredients
- 1 Frozen Banana

- ½ C. Orange Juice
- 1 Gala Apple
- ¼ C. Milk

Directions

1. Chop the banana and apple. Place ingredients in the blender and pulse until smooth.

Nutritional Information

Serving Size: ½ Recipe

Calories: 132

Calories from Fat: 9

Nutrient	Grams/mg	% Based on 2,000 Calorie Diet
Total Fat	1g	2%
Saturated Fat	0.5g	2%
Cholesterol	2mg	<1%
Sodium	14mg	<1%
Potassium	455mg	13%
Total Carbohydrates	30.9g	10%
Dietary Fiber	3.3g	13%
Protein	2.3g	5%
Sugars	21g	
Vitamin A		5%
Vitamin C		66%
Calcium		6%
Iron		4%
Thiamin		11%
Niacin		8%
Vitamin B6		18%
Magnesium		11%
Folate		19%

Banana Flaxseed Smoothie

Photo courtesy of Brian Everett at Flickr.com

Servings: 1

Prep: 10 Minutes

Ready In: 10 Minutes

Ingredients
- ½ C. Milk
- ½ C. Fat-Free Yogurt
- ½ Frozen Banana

- 2 Tbsp. Protein Supplement
- 1 ½ Tbsp. Flax Seed
- 1 tsp. Honey
- ½ C. Frozen Strawberries

Directions

1. Chop the banana.
2. Add the remainder of the ingredients and pulse until smooth.

Nutritional Information

Serving Size: 1 Recipe

Calories: 345

Calories from Fat: 51

Nutrient	Grams/mg	% Based on 2,000 Calorie Diet
Total Fat	5.6g	9%
Saturated Fat	0.4g	2%
Cholesterol	5mg	2%
Sodium	271mg	11%
Potassium	953mg	27%
Total Carbohydrates	5.9g	18%
Dietary Fiber	10.2g	41%
Protein	26.2g	52%
Sugars	33.9g	
Vitamin A		7%
Vitamin C		86%
Calcium		66%
Iron		106%
Thiamin		15%
Niacin		74
Vitamin B6		43%
Magnesium		26%

Folate		46%

Chocolate Banana Smoothie

Photo courtesy of donmarvin at Flickr.com

Servings: 1

Prep: 10 Minutes

Ready In: 10 Minutes

Ingredients

- 1 Banana

- 1 Tbsp. Chocolate Syrup
- 1 C. Milk
- 1 C. Ice

Directions

1. Chop the banana and place in the blender with the remainder of the ingredients. Pulse until smooth.

Nutritional Information

Serving Size: 1 Recipe

Calories: 279

Calories from Fat: 49

Nutrient	Grams/mg	% Based on 2,000 Calorie Diet
Total Fat	5.4g	8%
Saturated Fat	3.3g	16%
Cholesterol	20mg	7%
Sodium	122mg	5%
Potassium	833mg	23%
Total Carbohydrates	50.6g	16%
Dietary Fiber	3.6g	14%
Protein	9.7g	19%
Sugars	35.2g	
Vitamin A		11%
Vitamin C		18%
Calcium		38%
Iron		8%
Thiamin		15%
Niacin		22%
Vitamin B6		33%
Magnesium		26%
Folate		20%

Pineapple and Banana Smoothie

Photo courtesy of sylviemccracken at Flickr.com

Servings: 1

Prep: 10 Minutes

Ready In: 10 Minutes

Ingredients

- 4 Ice Cubes
- ¼ Fresh Pineapple
- 1 Banana
- 1 C. Pineapple Juice

Directions

1. Chop the banana and pineapple.
2. Place ingredients in the blender and pulse until smooth.

Nutritional Information

Serving Size: 1 Recipe

Calories: 313

Calories from Fat: 8

Nutrient	Grams/mg	% Based on 2,000 Calorie Diet
Total Fat	0.9g	1%
Saturated Fat	0.2g	<1%
Cholesterol	0mg	0%
Sodium	10mg	<1%
Potassium	941mg	26%
Total Carbohydrates	78.7g	25%
Dietary Fiber	5.7g	23%
Protein	3g	6%
Sugars	53.2g	
Vitamin A		3%
Vitamin C		155%
Calcium		7%
Iron		15%
Thiamin		31%
Niacin		19%

Vitamin B6		55%
Magnesium		29%
Folate		52%

Chapter Three – Strawberry Smoothies

Strawberries are high in vitamin C, so add these smoothies to your diet during the winter if you want to beat the flu bug going around the office. Be sure to hull the tops before you process them! Although, the extra bit of green won't hurt you.

Kiwi Strawberry Smoothie

Photo courtesy of Ellie W. at Flickr.com

Servings: 2

Prep: 10 Minutes

Ready In: 10 Minutes

Ingredients

- 1 Banana
- 6 Strawberries
- 1 Kiwi
- ½ C. Vanilla Frozen Yogurt
- ¾ C. Pineapple and Orange Juice

Directions

1. Chop the banana.
2. Place ingredients in the blender and pulse until smooth.

Nutritional Information

Serving Size: ½ Recipe

Calories: 204

Calories from Fat: 5

Nutrient	Grams/mg	% Based on 2,000 Calorie Diet
Total Fat	0.5g	<1%
Saturated Fat	0.1g	<1%
Cholesterol	2mg	<1%
Sodium	34mg	1%
Potassium	385mg	11%
Total Carbohydrates	48.1g	16%
Dietary Fiber	3.4g	14%
Protein	4.3g	9%
Sugars	32.1g	
Vitamin A		2%
Vitamin C		129%
Calcium		15%

Iron		4%
Thiamin		4%
Niacin		7%
Vitamin B6		16%
Magnesium		10%
Folate		17%

Red, White and Blue Fruit Smoothie

Photo courtesy of meghensley at Flickr.com

Servings: 1

Prep: 10 Minutes

Ready In: 10 Minutes

Ingredients

- ½ Banana
- 2 Large Strawberries
- ¼ C. Blueberries

- ½ C. Milk
- 1 tsp. Vanilla Extract
- 2 Tbsp. Vanilla Yogurt
- 2 Ice Cubes

Directions

1. Chop the banana and strawberries. Place everything in the blender except the ice cubes and blend until smooth.
2. Pour over ice cubes.

Nutritional Information

Serving Size: 1 Recipe

Calories: 192

Calories from Fat: 29

Nutrient	Grams/mg	% Based on 2,000 Calorie Diet
Total Fat	3.2g	5%
Saturated Fat	1.9g	9%
Cholesterol	11mg	4%
Sodium	73mg	3%
Potassium	583mg	16%
Total Carbohydrates	34g	11%
Dietary Fiber	3.4g	13%
Protein	6.8g	14%
Sugars	24.2g	
Vitamin A		6%
Vitamin C		52%
Calcium		26%
Iron		5%
Thiamin		12%
Niacin		15%
Vitamin B6		22%
Magnesium		16%

Folate		19%

Strawberry Watermelon Smoothie

Photo courtesy of Elina Innanen at Flickr.com

Servings: 1

Prep: 10 Minutes

Ready In: 10 Minutes

Ingredients

- 1 ½ C. Frozen Strawberries
- 1 ½ C. Frozen Diced Watermelon
- ¼ C. Cream
- ¼ C. Plain Yogurt
- 2 Tbsp. Orange Juice
- 1 Tbsp. White Sugar
- ¼ tsp. Vanilla Extract

Directions

1. Place all ingredients in the blender and pulse until smooth.

Nutritional Information

Serving Size: 1 Recipe

Calories: 494

Calories from Fat: 214

Nutrient	Grams/mg	% Based on 2,000 Calorie Diet
Total Fat	23.7g	37%
Saturated Fat	14.4g	72%
Cholesterol	85mg	28%
Sodium	75mg	3%
Potassium	998mg	28%
Total Carbohydrates	69.3g	22%
Dietary Fiber	7.6g	32%
Protein	7.5g	15%
Sugars	48.9g	
Vitamin A		48%
Vitamin C		28%
Calcium		38%
Iron		32%
Thiamin		32%
Niacin		25%

Vitamin B6		16%
Magnesium		45%
Folate		19%

Asian Pear Strawberry Smoothie

Photo courtesy of Megan at Flickr.com

Servings: 2

Prep: 10 Minutes

Ready In: 10 Minutes

Ingredients

- ½ C. Ice
- 1 Asian Pear
- 2 Strawberries
- 2/3 C. Vanilla Fat-Free Yogurt
- ¼ C. Fat-Free Milk
- 2 tsp. White Sugar

Directions

2. Dice pear and strawberries.

3. Place ingredients in blender and pulse until smooth.

Nutritional Information

Serving Size: ½ Recipe

Calories: 164

Calories from Fat: 5

Nutrient	Grams/mg	% Based on 2,000 Calorie Diet
Total Fat	0.5g	<1%
Saturated Fat	0.1g	<1%
Cholesterol	2mg	<1%
Sodium	71mg	3%
Potassium	429mg	12%
Total Carbohydrates	36g	12%
Dietary Fiber	5.3g	21%
Protein	6g	12%
Sugars	30.5g	
Vitamin A		1%
Vitamin C		27%
Calcium		24%
Iron		2%
Thiamin		3%
Niacin		9%
Vitamin B6		6%
Magnesium		11%
Folate		14%

Strawberry Milkshake

Photo courtesy of Celia Edell at Flickr.com

Servings: 1

Prep: 10 Minutes

Ready In: 10 Minutes

Ingredients

- 4 oz. Strawberries
- 1 C. Milk

- 1 Tbsp. Honey
- 6 Ice Cubes

Directions

1. Hull strawberries.
2. Place ingredients in the blender and process until smooth.

Nutritional Information

Serving Size: 1 Recipe

Calories: 222

Calories from Fat: 46

Nutrient	Grams/mg	% Based on 2,000 Calorie Diet
Total Fat	5.1g	8%
Saturated Fat	3.1g	15%
Cholesterol	20mg	7%
Sodium	106mg	4%
Potassium	550mg	15%
Total Carbohydrates	37.3g	12%
Dietary Fiber	2.3g	9%
Protein	8.9g	18%
Sugars	34.1g	
Vitamin A		9%
Vitamin C		111%
Calcium		39%
Iron		6%
Thiamin		12%
Niacin		18%
Vitamin B6		9%
Magnesium		15%
Folate		22%

Chapter Four – Orange Smoothies

Also very high in vitamin C and folate, oranges are great year round. They're especially good to add to morning smoothies for that extra boost of energy.

Gloomy Day Smoothie

Photo courtesy of Paige MacKenzie at Flickr.com

Servings: 4

Prep: 10 Minutes

Ready In: 10 Minutes

Ingredients

- 1 Mango
- 1 Banana
- 1 C. Orange Juice
- 1 C. Vanilla Yogurt, Non-Fat

Directions

1. Peel and dice mango and banana.
2. Place ingredients in the blender and pulse until smooth.

Nutritional Information

Serving Size: ¼ Recipe

Calories: 151

Calories from Fat: 4

Nutrient	Grams/mg	% Based on 2,000 Calorie Diet
Total Fat	0.5g	<1%
Saturated Fat	0.2g	<1%
Cholesterol	<1mg	<1%
Sodium	44mg	2%
Potassium	480mg	13%
Total Carbohydrates	34.6g	11%
Dietary Fiber	2g	8%
Protein	4.2g	8%
Sugars	28.2g	
Vitamin A		11%
Vitamin C		82%
Calcium		15%
Iron		3%

Thiamin		10%
Niacin		10%
Vitamin B6		16%
Magnesium		11%
Folate		22%

Orange Smoothie

Photo courtesy of SynergyByDesign at Flickr.com

Servings: 4

Prep: 10 Minutes

Ready In: 10 Minutes

Ingredients

- 1 Quart Strawberries
- 1 Banana
- 2 Peaches

- 1 C. Orange-Peach-Mango Juice
- 2 C. Ice

Directions

1. Hull the strawberries, cut up the banana into pieces and take the pit out of the peaches.
2. Throw everything into the blender and pulse until smooth.

Nutritional Information

Serving Size: ¼ Recipe

Calories: 118

Calories from Fat: 5

Nutrient	Grams/mg	% Based on 2,000 Calorie Diet
Total Fat	0.6g	<1%
Saturated Fat	0.1g	<1%
Cholesterol	0mg	0%
Sodium	16mg	<1%
Potassium	443mg	12%
Total Carbohydrates	28.5g	9%
Dietary Fiber	3.8g	15%
Protein	1.6g	3%
Sugars	19.6g	
Vitamin A		<1%
Vitamin C		215%
Calcium		4%
Iron		7%
Thiamin		6%
Niacin		8%
Vitamin B6		11%
Magnesium		11%
Folate		24%

Orange Sunrise Smoothie

Photo courtesy of Vita Mix at Flickr.com

Servings: 2

Prep: 10 Minutes

Ready In: 10 Minutes

Ingredients

- ½ C. Orange Juice
- 1 Banana
- 1 Peach
- ½ C. Honeydew Melon
- 8 oz. Orange Yogurt
- 1 tsp. White Sugar
- ½ C. Ice

Directions

1. Peel and chop the banana, peach, and melon.
2. Place ingredients in the blender and pulse until smooth.

Nutritional Information

Serving Size: ½ Recipe

Calories: 239

Calories from Fat: 11

Nutrient	Grams/mg	% Based on 2,000 Calorie Diet
Total Fat	1.3g	2%
Saturated Fat	0.5g	3%
Cholesterol	9mg	3%
Sodium	69mg	3%
Potassium	670mg	19%
Total Carbohydrates	52g	17%
Dietary Fiber	2g	8%
Protein	8g	12%
Sugars	41.4g	
Vitamin A		4%
Vitamin C		74%
Calcium		19%
Iron		4%
Thiamin		12%

Niacin		7%
Vitamin B6		18%
Magnesium		10%
Folate		22%

Orange Ginger Smoothie

Photo courtesy of .thomas alexander at Flickr.com

Servings: 1

Prep: 10 Minutes

Ready In: 10 Minutes

Ingredients
- 1 Orange
- 2 Carrots
- ½ C. Red Grapes

- ½ C. Ice Cubes
- ¼ C. Water
- 1" Piece of Fresh Ginger

Directions

1. Peel and dice the orange and chop up the carrots.
2. Place the ingredients in the blender and pulse until smooth.

Nutritional Information

Serving Size: 1 Recipe

Calories: 120

Calories from Fat: 8

Nutrient	Grams/mg	% Based on 2,000 Calorie Diet
Total Fat	0.2g	1%
Saturated Fat	0.2g	1%
Cholesterol	0mg	0%
Sodium	107mg	4%
Potassium	634mg	18%
Total Carbohydrates	29g	9%
Dietary Fiber	4.9g	20%
Protein	2g	4%
Sugars	20.3g	
Vitamin A		482%
Vitamin C		29%
Calcium		8%
Iron		7%
Thiamin		21%
Niacin		15%
Vitamin B6		18%
Magnesium		9%
Folate		17%

Orange Cinnamon Smoothie

Photo courtesy of theblonderunner1 at Flickr.com

Servings: 4

Prep: 10 Minutes

Ready In: 10 Minutes

Ingredients

- 6 C. Orange Juice
- 3 C. Vanilla Yogurt
- 3 Oranges
- ½ tsp. Ground Cinnamon

Directions

1. Peel and segment the oranges.
2. Place all ingredients into the blender and process until smooth.

Nutritional Information

Serving Size: ¼ Recipe

Calories: 389

Calories from Fat: 29

Nutrient	Grams/mg	% Based on 2,000 Calorie Diet
Total Fat	3.2g	5%
Saturated Fat	1.6g	8%
Cholesterol	9mg	3%
Sodium	125mg	5%
Potassium	1397mg	39%
Total Carbohydrates	80.5g	26%
Dietary Fiber	4.2g	17%
Protein	13g	26%
Sugars	69.5g	
Vitamin A		23%
Vitamin C		435%
Calcium		52%
Iron		10%
Thiamin		53%
Niacin		25%
Vitamin B6		20%
Magnesium		30%
Folate		96%

Chapter Five ~ Blueberry Smoothies

It's no secret that blueberries are excellent for heart health, and they're high in vitamin C, too. Blueberries are an excellent choice for any smoothie due to their natural antioxidants.

Very Berry Blueberry Smoothie

Photo courtesy of Will S at Flickr.com

Servings: 3

Prep: 10 Minutes

Ready In: 10 Minutes

Ingredients

- 1 Banana
- 1 Kiwi
- ¾ C. Blueberries
- 1 C. Ice
- 8 oz. Vanilla Yogurt

Directions

1. Peel and dice the banana and kiwi.
2. Place the ingredients in the blender and pulse until smooth.

Nutritional Information

Serving Size: 1/3 Recipe

Calories: 135

Calories from Fat: 12

Nutrient	Grams/mg	% Based on 2,000 Calorie Diet
Total Fat	1.3g	2%
Saturated Fat	0.7g	3%
Cholesterol	4mg	1%
Sodium	54mg	2%
Potassium	414mg	12%
Total Carbohydrates	28.4g	9%
Dietary Fiber	2.7g	11%
Protein	4.7g	9%
Sugars	21.1g	
Vitamin A		2%
Vitamin C		52%

Calcium		18%
Iron		3%
Thiamin		7%
Niacin		8%
Vitamin B6		13%
Magnesium		11%
Folate		14%

Blueberry Smoothie

Photo courtesy of Sue Berger at Flickr.com

Servings: 2

Prep: 10 Minutes

Ready In: 10 Minutes

Ingredients

- 1 C. Blueberries
- 8 oz. Plain Yogurt
- ¾ C. Milk
- 2 Tbsp. White Sugar
- ½ tsp. Vanilla Extract
- 1/8 tsp. Ground Nutmeg

Directions

1. Place all ingredients and process until smooth.

Nutritional Information

Serving Size: ½ Recipe

Calories: 211

Calories from Fat: 35

Nutrient	Grams/mg	% Based on 2,000 Calorie Diet
Total Fat	3.9g	6%
Saturated Fat	2.4g	12%
Cholesterol	14mg	5%
Sodium	118mg	5%
Potassium	461mg	13%
Total Carbohydrates	35.5g	11%
Dietary Fiber	1.8g	7%
Protein	9.5g	19%
Sugars	32.2g	
Vitamin A		5%
Vitamin C		14%
Calcium		40%
Iron		3%
Thiamin		12%

Niacin		13%
Vitamin B6		8%
Magnesium		12%
Folate		12%

Razzy Blue Smoothie

Photo courtesy Sylvia at Flickr.com

Servings: 3

Prep: 10 Minutes

Ready In: 10 Minutes

Ingredients

- 2 Bananas
- 16 Almonds
- ¼ C. Rolled Oats
- 1 Tbsp. Flaxseed meal

- 1 C. Frozen Blueberries
- 1 C. Raspberry Yogurt
- ¼ C. Grape Juice
- 1 C. Buttermilk

Directions

1. Peel and chop the banana.
2. Place all ingredients in the blender and process until smooth.

Nutritional Information

Serving Size: 1/3 Recipe

Calories: 262

Calories from Fat: 59

Nutrient	Grams/mg	% Based on 2,000 Calorie Diet
Total Fat	6.5g	10%
Saturated Fat	1.4g	7%
Cholesterol	8mg	3%
Sodium	142mg	6%
Potassium	540mg	15%
Total Carbohydrates	44.5g	14%
Dietary Fiber	4.8g	19%
Protein	8.8g	18%
Sugars	30.3g	
Vitamin A		2%
Vitamin C		11%
Calcium		29%
Iron		11%
Thiamin		14%
Niacin		16%
Vitamin B6		15%
Magnesium		22%

Folate		12%

For Your Heart Blueberry Smoothie

Photo courtesy of nils gore at Flickr.com

Servings: 2

Prep: 10 Minutes

Ready In: 10 Minutes

Ingredients

- 1 C. Blueberries
- ¾ C. Pomegranate Juice
- ½ C. Plain Greek Yogurt
- ½ C. Milk
- ½ C. Rolled Oats
- ¼ C. Sugar
- 1 tsp. Ground Cinnamon

Directions

1. Place all ingredients in the blender and process until smooth.

Nutritional Information

Serving Size: ½ Recipe

Calories: 252

Calories from Fat: 25

Nutrient	Grams/mg	% Based on 2,000 Calorie Diet
Total Fat	2.8g	4%
Saturated Fat	1.1g	6%
Cholesterol	4mg	1%
Sodium	50mg	2%
Potassium	230mg	6%
Total Carbohydrates	53.3g	17%
Dietary Fiber	4.4g	18%
Protein	10.1g	20%
Sugars	25.4g	
Vitamin A		3%
Vitamin C		12%
Calcium		13%
Iron		12%
Thiamin		21%
Niacin		13%
Vitamin B6		5%
Magnesium		14%
Folate		8%

Almond Butter Blueberry Smoothie

Photo courtesy of Marji Beach at Flickr.com

Servings: 2

Prep: 10 Minutes

Ready In: 10 Minutes

Ingredients

- 1 C. Almond milk
- 1 C. Blueberries
- 4 Ice Cubes
- 1 Scoop Vanilla Protein Powder

- 1 Tbsp. Almond Butter
- 1 Tbsp. Chia Seeds

Directions

1. Place all ingredients in the blender and blend until smooth.

Nutritional Information

Serving Size: ½ Recipe

Calories: 230

Calories from Fat: 73

Nutrient	Grams/mg	% Based on 2,000 Calorie Diet
Total Fat	8.1g	12%
Saturated Fat	1.2g	6%
Cholesterol	6mg	2%
Sodium	225mg	9%
Potassium	219mg	6%
Total Carbohydrates	20g	6%
Dietary Fiber	4g	16%
Protein	21.6g	43%
Sugars	12g	
Vitamin A		6%
Vitamin C		13%
Calcium		20%
Iron		11%
Thiamin		8%
Niacin		12%
Vitamin B6		4%
Magnesium		14%
Folate		8%

Chapter Six – Mango Smoothies

Did you know that mangoes are almost nutritiously comparable to an orange? That's why they're great for breakfast smoothies and for your overall health.

Honey Mango Smoothie

Photo courtesy of thebearfootbaker at Flickr.com

Servings: 2

Prep: 10 Minutes

Ready In: 10 Minutes

Ingredients

- 1 Mango
- 1 Tbsp. White Sugar
- 2 Tbsp. Honey
- 1 C. Nonfat Milk
- 1 tsp. Lemon Juice
- 1 C. Ice Cubes

Directions

1. Peel and dice mango.
2. Place all ingredients in the blender and pulse until smooth.

Nutritional Information

Serving Size: ½ Recipe

Calories: 198

Calories from Fat: 3

Nutrient	Grams/mg	% Based on 2,000 Calorie Diet
Total Fat	0.4g	<1%
Saturated Fat	0.1g	<1%
Cholesterol	2mg	<1%
Sodium	58mg	2%
Potassium	368mg	10%
Total Carbohydrates	47.5g	15%
Dietary Fiber	1.9g	8%
Protein	4.7g	9%
Sugars	44.9g	
Vitamin A		21%
Vitamin C		50%
Calcium		21%
Iron		3%
Thiamin		10%
Niacin		13%

Vitamin B6		12%
Magnesium		9%
Folate		12%

Vanilla Banana Mango Smoothie

Photo courtesy of M. Klasan at Flickr.com

Servings: 2

Prep: 10 Minutes

Ready In: 10 Minutes

Ingredients

- ¼ C. Orange Juice
- 1 Mango
- 1 Frozen Banana
- 2 Baby Carrots

- 6 oz. Vanilla Yogurt
- 2 Ice Cubes
- 1 tsp. Ground Ginger

Directions
1. Peel and dice the mango and slice the banana.
2. Place all ingredients in the blender and pulse until smooth.

Nutritional Information

Serving Size: ½ Recipe

Calories: 192

Calories from Fat: 14

Nutrient	Grams/mg	% Based on 2,000 Calorie Diet
Total Fat	1.6g	2%
Saturated Fat	0.8g	4%
Cholesterol	4mg	1%
Sodium	62mg	2%
Potassium	596mg	17%
Total Carbohydrates	42.1g	14%
Dietary Fiber	3.1g	13%
Protein	5.5g	11%
Sugars	32.8g	
Vitamin A		23%
Vitamin C		70%
Calcium		20%
Iron		5%
Thiamin		13%
Niacin		13%
Vitamin B6		24%
Magnesium		15%
Folate		23%

Tropical Sunshine Smoothie

Photo courtesy of nooschi at Flickr.com

Servings: 2

Prep: 10 Minutes

Ready In: 10 Minutes

Ingredients

- 1 Banana
- ½ C. Orange Juice
- ½ C. Fresh Mango
- ½ C. Pineapple
- ½ C. Coconut Water
- ½ tsp. Lime Juice
- 1 Sprig Chocolate Mint

Directions

1. Peel and dice the banana, mango, and pineapple.
2. Place all ingredients in the blender and process until smooth.

Nutritional Information

Serving Size: ½ Recipe

Calories: 140

Calories from Fat: 5

Nutrient	Grams/mg	% Based on 2,000 Calorie Diet
Total Fat	0.6g	<1%
Saturated Fat	0.2g	1%
Cholesterol	0mg	0%
Sodium	66mg	3%
Potassium	599mg	17%
Total Carbohydrates	34.8g	11%
Dietary Fiber	3.6g	15%
Protein	2g	4%
Sugars	22.6g	
Vitamin A		10%
Vitamin C		117%
Calcium		5%
Iron		7%
Thiamin		16%
Niacin		10%
Vitamin B6		23%
Magnesium		17%
Folate		26%

Coconut Banana Mango Smoothie

Photo courtesy of Tasty Yummies at Flickr.com

Servings: 2

Prep: 10 Minutes

Ready In: 10 Minutes

Ingredients

- 1 Mango
- 1 ½ Bananas
- ½ C. Coconut Milk
- ½ C. Water
- 4 Ice Cubes
- 1 Tbsp. White Sugar
- 1 tsp. Coconut Extract
- ½ tsp. Lime Zest

Directions

1. Peel and dice the mango and banana.
2. Place all ingredients in the blender and process until smooth.

Nutritional Information

Serving Size: ½ Recipe

Calories: 268

Calories from Fat: 113

Nutrient	Grams/mg	% Based on 2,000 Calorie Diet
Total Fat	12.5g	19%
Saturated Fat	10.8g	54%
Cholesterol	0mg	0%
Sodium	13mg	<1%
Potassium	562mg	16%
Total Carbohydrates	40.9g	13%
Dietary Fiber	4.3g	17%
Protein	2.5g	5%
Sugars	28.2g	
Vitamin A		13%
Vitamin C		49%

Calcium		3%
Iron		22%
Thiamin		10%
Niacin		14%
Vitamin B6		28%
Magnesium		21%
Folate		20%

Carrot Cake Smoothie

Photo courtesy of Tasty Yummies at Flickr.com

Servings: 1

Prep: 10 Minutes

Ready In: 10 Minutes

Ingredients

- 1 Carrot
- ¼ Mango
- 1 Peach
- ¼ C. Soy Milk
- 1 Tbsp. Ground Cinnamon
- 1 tsp. Ground Allspice
- 1 tsp. Ground Ginger

Directions

1. Dice the carrot and peel and dice the mango.
2. Place all ingredients in the blender and process until smooth.

Nutritional Information

Serving Size: 1 Recipe

Calories: 151

Calories from Fat: 15

Nutrient	Grams/mg	% Based on 2,000 Calorie Diet
Total Fat	1.7g	3%
Saturated Fat	0.3g	1%
Cholesterol	0mg	0%
Sodium	89mg	4%
Potassium	48mg	14%
Total Carbohydrates	34g	11%
Dietary Fiber	7.4g	30%
Protein	3.5g	7%
Sugars	20.2g	
Vitamin A		248%
Vitamin C		122%
Calcium		18%

Iron		16%
Thiamin		23%
Niacin		16%
Vitamin B6		15%
Magnesium		15%
Folate		18%

Chapter Seven – Dessert Smoothies

Who doesn't love dessert? And when it comes in a smoothie form, it will most likely contain less fat. Go ahead and enjoy your dessert and know that you're getting a lot of vitamins along with it!

Strawberry Shortcake Smoothie

Photo courtesy of msihua at Flickr.com

Servings: 3

Prep: 10 Minutes

Ready In: 10 Minutes

Ingredients

- 2 C. Nonfat Plain Yogurt
- 2 C. Milk
- 2 C. Frozen Strawberries
- 6 Shortbread Cookies
- 4 tsp. Sugar
- 1 tsp. Vanilla Extract
- 6 Tbsp. Whey Protein Powder

Directions

1. Crumble the shortbread cookies into the blender.
2. Place the remaining ingredients in the blender and pulse until smooth.

Nutritional Information

Serving Size: 1/3 Recipe

Calories: 363

Calories from Fat: 79

Nutrient	Grams/mg	% Based on 2,000 Calorie Diet
Total Fat	8.7g	13%
Saturated Fat	3g	15%
Cholesterol	19mg	6%
Sodium	259mg	10%
Potassium	844mg	24%
Total Carbohydrates	40.1g	13%
Dietary Fiber	2.2g	9%
Protein	32.9g	66%
Sugars	29.3g	
Vitamin A		7%
Vitamin C		111%
Calcium		67%

Iron		14%
Thiamin		16%
Niacin		21%
Vitamin B6		13%
Magnesium		23%
Folate		30%

Apple Pie Smoothie

Photo courtesy of Tasty Yummies at Flickr.com

Servings: 2

Prep: 10 Minutes

Ready In: 10 Minutes

Ingredients

- 12 oz. Vanilla Yogurt
- ½ C. Pumpkin Pie Filling
- 1 Banana
- 2 C. Apple Juice
- 1 tsp. Ground Cinnamon
- 1 Dash Ground Nutmeg

Directions

1. Slice the banana.
2. Place the rest of the ingredients in the blender and process until smooth.

Nutritional Information

Serving Size: ½ Recipe

Calories: 389

Calories from Fat: 26

Nutrient	Grams/mg	% Based on 2,000 Calorie Diet
Total Fat	2.9g	4%
Saturated Fat	1.7g	8%
Cholesterol	8mg	3%
Sodium	261mg	10%
Potassium	978mg	24%
Total Carbohydrates	84.9g	27%
Dietary Fiber	8.1g	32%
Protein	10g	20%
Sugars	57.9g	
Vitamin A		114%
Vitamin C		19%
Calcium		44%
Iron		20%
Thiamin		16%

Niacin		15%
Vitamin B6		30%
Magnesium		22%
Folate		30%

Chocolate Banana Peanut butter Smoothie

Photo courtesy of Tuppence at Flickr.com

Servings: 2

Prep: 10 Minutes

Ready In: 10 Minutes

Ingredients

- 2 C. Ice
- 2 C. Chocolate Soy Milk

- 1 Banana
- 2 Tbsp. Peanut Butter

Directions

1. Peel and slice the banana and place in the blender.
2. Place the remaining ingredients in the blender and process until smooth.

Nutritional Information

Serving Size: ½ Recipe

Calories: 315

Calories from Fat: 82

Nutrient	Grams/mg	% Based on 2,000 Calorie Diet
Total Fat	9.2g	14%
Saturated Fat	1.8g	9%
Cholesterol	0mg	0%
Sodium	82mg	3%
Potassium	351mg	10%
Total Carbohydrates	58.2g	19%
Dietary Fiber	2.7g	11%
Protein	10.2g	20%
Sugars	9.8g	
Vitamin A		<1%
Vitamin C		10%
Calcium		16%
Iron		15%
Thiamin		4%
Niacin		54%
Vitamin B6		21%
Magnesium		16%
Folate		14%

Cremesicle Smoothie

Photo courtesy of Shekhar Mehta at Flickr.com

Servings: 2

Prep: 10 Minutes

Ready In: 10 Minutes

Ingredients

- 1 C. Orange Juice
- 1 C. Milk
- 1 C. Ice
- 1 tsp. White Sugar

Directions

1. Place all ingredients in the blender and process until smooth.

Nutritional Information

Serving Size: ½ Recipe

Calories: 125

Calories from Fat: 24

Nutrient	Grams/mg	% Based on 2,000 Calorie Diet
Total Fat	2.7g	4%
Saturated Fat	1.6g	8%
Cholesterol	10mg	3%
Sodium	53mg	2%
Potassium	432mg	12%
Total Carbohydrates	20.7g	7%
Dietary Fiber	0.2g	<1%
Protein	4.9g	10%
Sugars	18.2g	
Vitamin A		10%
Vitamin C		104%
Calcium		20%
Iron		3%
Thiamin		16%
Niacin		11%
Vitamin B6		6%
Magnesium		10%
Folate		24%

Molasses Spice Smoothie

Photo courtesy of Stacy at Flickr.com

Servings: 2

Prep: 10 Minutes

Ready In: 10 Minutes

Ingredients

- 1 C. Milk
- ½ C. Oats
- ½ C. Ice Cubes
- 1 Frozen Banana
- 2 Tbsp. Molasses
- ½ tsp. Ground Ginger
- ½ tsp. Ground Cinnamon
- ¼ tsp. Vanilla Extract
- 1 Pinch Ground Cloves

Directions

1. Slice the banana and place in the blender.
2. Place remaining ingredients in the blender and process until smooth.

Nutritional Information

Serving Size: ½ Recipe

Calories: 247

Calories from Fat: 36

Nutrient	Grams/mg	% Based on 2,000 Calorie Diet
Total Fat	4g	6%
Saturated Fat	1.9g	9%
Cholesterol	10mg	3%
Sodium	62mg	2%
Potassium	745mg	21%
Total Carbohydrates	47.1g	15%
Dietary Fiber	3.9g	16%
Protein	7.3g	15%

Sugars	23.3g	
Vitamin A		5%
Vitamin C		8%
Calcium		26%
Iron		21%
Thiamin		23%
Niacin		18%
Vitamin B6		25%
Magnesium		38%
Folate		13%

Conclusion

Whether you need a meal on the go or you're just looking for something simple to whip up, smoothies are a great choice! Keep your ingredients frozen in the freezer and pull them out a few minutes before you want to give them a whirl, and you'll have a refreshing snack or meal in the summertime. Keep your ingredients at room temperature and it won't be so cold in the wintertime.

If you enjoyed some of the recipes in this book, please go to your online eBook provider and leave a positive review. It would be greatly appreciated

Thank you for reading!

With love and respect,

Printed in Great Britain
by Amazon

36133882R00056